The Future of Education

The Future of Education

Avery Nightingale

CONTENTS

1. Introduction — 1
2. Technology in Education — 3
3. Personalized Learning — 9
4. Global Collaboration — 15
5. Project-Based Learning — 21
6. Social and Emotional Learning — 25
7. STEAM Education — 31
8. Future Skills Development — 37
9. Inclusive Education — 43
10. Teacher Professional Development — 49

Copyright © 2024 by Avery Nightingale
All rights reserved. No part of this book may be reproduced in any manner whatsoever without written permission except in the case of brief quotations embodied in critical articles and reviews.
First Printing, 2024

1

Introduction

After identifying a selection of thought-leading trends about change that may impact schooling, we will outline how schools might act to ensure their own futures. Acknowledging that checking developing trends is an integral part of the planning activity, we maintain that change has the potential to be both challenging and exciting. In doing so, we identify various actions schools can take to meet their challenges head-on. This paper provides practical strategies for school leaders and governors to secure a minimalist future, providing original insight into the strategic future planning of your school. Our general approach is participant-centered and assumes the reader possesses some previous knowledge of the issue, so as not to overload this work.

This white paper puts forward the case for a futures-oriented approach to school development. Too often, current trends are framed as the beginning of the end for the future of schooling. In reality, the introduction of technology, demographic change, or increased mobility isn't an act of displacement, but the first chapter of a new beginning. In order to ensure that your school remains relevant and an appealing choice for futures-focused parents, an iterative, future-focused approach is essential.

2

Technology in Education

Research has shown that evidence-based training on how to use these tools successfully is necessary for their complete effective integration into our educational systems. This research supports that technology needs to be understood and used in context as one piece of the puzzle to drive the necessary change in our educational organizations currently in great need. This aligns with Michael Fullan's belief that educational innovations and technology will only work when connected to successful pedagogy and systemic change. "Change in technology, change in pedagogy, and change in organizations are not separate pieces." The Organization for Economic Co-operation and Development (OECD) believes that when used effectively, learning technology can also change the relative costs of different types of goods and services, persuasive evidence to shift educational leaders to think differently about the models for further learning.

In today's world, the integration of technology can be seen in many aspects of school life, from using technology to support learning in the classroom, through to online messaging and the use of individual devices such as mobile phones and school-owned devices. Worldwide, technology-based learning is everywhere with new applications, websites, platforms, interactions, communities, and opportunities appearing every day. With these opportunities, however, come potential challenges. While technology has the potential to greatly improve the quality of learning, teaching, and assessment, open up access to learning, assist in rethinking the time and place for teaching and learning, and provide many different avenues of support and tools to enhance learning, technology in isolation for any or all of these objectives does not guarantee any improvement.

2.1. Integration of Virtual Reality

The capability of visualizing and interacting with objects and concepts in immersive environments can offer education a new methodology to teach new content, to simulate real situations or to collaborate with other students. This is attractive not only to teachers but also to students, since it brings more incentive to learn new contents and most probably requires the development of learning processes more challenging than the traditional ones. In the era of experience economy, virtual reality is already a reality in schools. The market of VRH is expected to grow from 43M units in 2017 to 98M units in 2021. It is estimated that ca. 15M of these devices will be acquired by educational institutions in a 5-year period. Even if the potential of using virtual reality (VR) in the educational process is remarkable in global terms, it is in Brazil that it offers a high impact because of the suitability of educational practices according to the National Curricular Standards (PCN), of the strengthening of the student's argumentative capacity and to make the dynamics and the student's motivation significant.

Just a few years ago, virtual reality (VR) was something that seemed to be very unlikely to be available in schools in the near future. However, with the appearance of headsets like Oculus Rift or HTC Vive, VR has found its place in the education process. The virtual reality headsets (VRH) can be used to visualize educational content in a new manner. Beyond consuming pre-created educational content (e.g., a video), with virtual reality, students are able to experience a virtual environment as if it were the real world. Virtual reality adds interactivity to the 360° video, in which the viewer is limited to look around. The headset is represented by a mobile phone or a computer that is inserted into it (creating a head-mounted display). This allows students to visualize contents in a virtual environment by using the head movements (the rotation around the vertical and the horizontal axes) to look to the front, the side, the behind, above, or below. The efficiency of using virtual reality in education is not completely clear, but there are many indications that it could be a future path educators will want to explore more for various reasons.

2.2. Online Learning Platforms

In summary, current research does not provide a justification for widespread implementation of online instruction as a response to COVID-19. Most studies point to this conclusion, particularly in the primary and early-secondary grades. Nevertheless, such findings do not automatically apply to all possible new main or supplemental educational strategies, the contextual conditions in which they may be present, and education systems that are likely to apply in the short or long term. We must, however, be cautious before investing heavily in online learning platforms at the primary level.

Many online learning platforms had already been thriving in the years before COVID-19 hit, including Google Classroom, Seesaw, and Class DOJO among others. During the pandemic, many new ones have been launched, or older ones have been improved, including many specifically designed for online learning in the primary years, such as Google Tasks and Jamboard, Smart Learning Suite Online, and many others. Significantly, online learning platforms can help personalize instruction and assessment, promote individual agency and flexible pacing, conceptual understanding, and periodic project-based learning. The effectiveness of platforms appears to generally be enhanced when they involve content and task curation, continuous teacher feedback, accountability, and the setting of diligent learning expectations, among certain other criteria.

2.3. Artificial Intelligence in Education

The development and implementation of AI in education, however, is likely to develop unevenly, as richer schools and institutions in flexible education technology markets such as those in edtech, in the future, are deploying it more quickly than schools where investments are most needed. This raises concerns about the growing digital divide in education. The authors underscore the importance of using a clear, shared understanding of how technology can help educators, establishing best practices for using AI in education, and creating specific metrics to measure its impact to encourage greater investment in implementation planning of AI in education. Given the potential of AI, it is important that the education system ensures that AI makes learning more effective, rather than merely automating the teaching process. Rapid progress in AI, with possible side effects, will require public authorities and school operators to work together to ensure that responsible decisions are made about when and how to apply the technology that takes the specificities of learning and teaching into consideration. The authors highlight the possibility of using AI to guide and enhance research, for example in the design of virtual laboratories and in the analysis of large-scale data, and that more collaborative work would be beneficial for teachers, students, and institutions.

Artificial Intelligence (AI) has a central role to play in shaping the classrooms and learning processes of tomorrow. Organizations use AI to personalize learning experiences. It also helps students better understand complex concepts, teaches students personal initiative, and enables teachers to teach. IBM Watson is a suite of AI tools that can be applied to K-12 education, including personalized learning, teacher virtual assistants, and virtual tutors. Software such as Google's TensorFlow and the teaching machines of Carnegie Mellon University are democratizing the creation and implementation of such tutoring systems.

3

Personalized Learning

Examples such as education technology company, have partnerships with institutions such as the Colorado Community College System. The EdTech company recently announced a new initiative that merges their current stack with teacher-led networks and independent instructors, offering students and corporate clients a wider variety of courses. Others, like Silicon Schools in California, are integrating more robust technology solutions to support their personalized learning programs, using K-12 resources like online learning evolution videos, a competency-based progression, and acquiescent sites that focus on early literacy. Leading the charge in powerful personalized learning isn't just for the educational pioneers any longer; there's a drive for enhancing these modern and innovative methodologies in all types of educational institutions. This shift to cultivating is for individualized learning is occurring across all levels of education including K-12, higher education, corporate learning and vocational institutions.

Personalized learning is a tailor-made, highly flexible learning process that emphasizes student connection to the subject matter and extends the learning beyond the boundaries of the classroom. With smaller class sizes and various teaching formats – from traditional lecture to flipped classroom to peer learning – the personalized learning environment often aims to achieve a program that is individualized for the individual student. Its main goal is to empower students to be the owners of their educational journey, thus promoting the long-lasting success of individuals regardless of demographics, socio-economic status or geography. Technology companies are making headway on positioning themselves as the leaders within the personalized learning sector. With the collaborative education space on the rise, these companies are often adopting an "adopt-the-platform" approach, where their platforms are the backbone of personalized learning programs.

3.1. Adaptive Learning Programs

As it is always the case with technology-driven change, new technology becomes more sophisticated, more accepted, and better understood every year. The technology at work here is not so much the adaptive learning algorithm but rather the increased use of the internet. Billions of additional people (soon to include every human on this planet) are plugging into the same communication's backbone every day. The explosive use of information technologies is now doubling the scope and accessibility of this backbone every year (even as the technologies themselves compound at faster rates). This is in turn making the quantum of human knowledge geometrically expand every year. In time, adaptive learning will become more plain old learning. Four or five classroom hours every week will become education bubbles (to borrow a notion from Howard Buffett). Since the days of using stone tablets, the days of the chalkboard will soon come to pass. Then the days of the printed book. But for the first time in human history, the days of the school will soon come to pass.

3.1. Adaptive Learning Programs. Adaptive learning is an educational method that uses computer algorithms to modify instruction in real-time based on the information the algorithm is collecting.

This sounds like something out of a science fiction movie. However, many computer programs tailor questions to the individual's level based on the answers that individual gives (like in standardized testing). Adaptive learning takes this to the next level and can actually personalize education. There is considerable evidence to suggest that adaptive learning programs produce learning better than some forms of instructor-led instruction in many areas of education – trivial pursuits aside. In the last few years, the use of personalized education services have exploded online (as well). Adaptive learning companies are providing both college education and certificate prep education at levels of quality that exceed that of more traditional institutions such as the University of Phoenix.

3.2. Individualized Instruction

A key component of personalized instruction is meticulous evaluation of learner performance and progress, which will generate additional skills for learners. Monitoring the progress of millions of students in virtual learning environments generates enormous amounts of data on how students learn, how they perform in real time, and, from millions of students, on different ways how they learn most efficiently. Dubai students can take advantage of these metrics to understand their unique pathways to success. For example, as the system evaluates that students master a particular topic during instruction in the language they find most productive, the tool will proceed to present other learning materials to them in the same format. Similarly, if it is seen that students achieve a certain proficiency in collaborative inquiry, the program will allocate more time for small group activities. This constant analysis will be used to provide recommendations to students on what types of activities and approaches to choose to improve various tools and resources available to promote learning.

Classroom activities are also personalized: students move at their own pace through required assignments, show proficiency before moving to the next level, and can access online resources as an option between school years so they can quickly and easily refresh if necessary. Think of a class playing chess; there will be twenty chess games in progress at the same time, but each student makes moves independently of the others. If any of those students stumble on a subject, the coach is notified and can use this information to address the learning area in a sequential manner in the chess game. As many schools are overwhelmed with learners, this approach is designed to lessen the segregation model in schools; now, every student will have their own learning puzzle, designed for them. Inquiry-based learning models, individualized instruction, development opportunities, and rapid feedback mechanisms will allow them to regularly gain knowledge and future capabilities to help them adapt to new challenges.

3.3. Competency-Based Education

This transformation re-focused school districts (and later, colleges) on the student - and both learning and teaching applied to their individualized context. Professional development debates shifted from what teachers "should" know (the instructional script) to the relationships learners had with the academic content. Learning was conceived as competency-based and built to foster the unique development of a child into a productive actor within a community and the nation. The impetus was reactive, as all such changes are; reshaping a very complex organization like a public school district was an arduous task, akin to turning an aircraft carrier without diminishing the ability of the civilians onboard to carry out their regular work. Decades in, as data begins to paint the picture of the success (or alternative) of such designs, we discern observable trends across the implementation of competency-based education (CBE).

Competency-based education has steadily gained ground over the last thirty years in school districts across the collective. The theory was advanced, and the practice codified, by Marzano and his colleagues who took the approach of shifting the design of instructional practices from teacher-centered to student-centered classrooms in research. In doing so, they identified a specific architecture of standards (outcomes), curriculum (learning design), assessments, reporting, and targeted instruction that distinguished this "new" personalization from that of the past - and opened the door for IT to transform education into the learner-focused system that is now some 3 decades later.

4

Global Collaboration

Collaboration is now an essential skill for success in the 21st century. Enhanced global communication and collaboration tools have given students opportunities to engage with peers around the world. Today's students can, and should, learn with the world and about the world. Even at a local level, schools are working with each other to share resources and knowledge. For instance, the World Economic Forum and Global Education & Leadership Foundation (tGELF) have formed the first-ever public-private partnership to bring their values-based learning programs into just about 200 Haileyburys. In the United States, the 'NCLB Waivers' program had states competing for federal funds by promising to improve educational spaces through well-crafted leadership that aligned with students' personal growth as well as faculty members' certifications.

The right kind of global collaboration and problem-solving can take students on a fascinating journey around the world, all the while supporting the development of such 21st-century skills as critical thinking and collaboration. Tools such as Skype have made these connections easier and more powerful than ever. And while not every student has access to these promising technologies, the numbers are rising rapidly. For instance, despite a ban on social networking, 60% of low-income students in Iran use the popular Facebook.

4.1. International Exchange Programs

The above story—the International Exchange Program as narrated in 2072—is based on elements in a vision for holistic education systems across the world, elements that extend beyond the social goals of UNESCO MGIEP to develop learners' minds. These elements are seven transnational skills (creativity, digital literacy, critical thinking, global citizenship, communication, collaboration, leadership) and then character outcomes that foster in a learner those skills. Structures such as Exchange Visits and Exchanges between teachers and students that have these goals in mind are called Global Collaboration Projects and under our vision are scaled to something we call the Mirabili trianguli – a fully transnational classroom of twenty students from across the world. The courage to try, fail, persist, and innovate towards a common goal or a personal one is achieved when students from vastly socio-economic backgrounds become a team, when learners valued from word one as innovators are asked to lead their classmates to mastery on class goals from across the world.

The year is 2072. Sally is nineteen and steps off an airplane in Nairobi. She sits next to a Maasai girl in her classroom and struggles with math in a mud hut. The experiences and the friendships made across the world have added up to much more. Sally walks back home to Shanghai with a clear sense of why she wants to get into computer programming, and not because she was told it was the right thing to do, but because she learned that the community, 7,019 kilometers away, valued her trust, leadership, and action around that innovation the most. She doesn't know if her new friends will become tomato farmers, but she's certain that they have agricultural innovations in their minds to alleviate hunger and poverty. Sally's exchange program had not only taught her, it had transformed her character, her confidence, and her drive. She was ready for the world.

The year is 2072, and 19-year-old Sally walks into a packed conference hall in Shanghai. She takes her seat next to a range of students from other countries waiting to hear the announcement on sustainable energy made by the Maasai girl she once sat with, the one now with profits but Sachet Solar Lamps. She is elated, not many 19-year-old girls would be able to say they were just capable of enhancing technology sharing with a community in rural Kenya!

4.2. Cross-Cultural Learning

Despite the growth of cross-cultural learning experiences, it is important to point out that not all can afford such life-changing experiences which can be a life-altering educational experience, even for those with relatively mild disabilities. Poverty cannot be allowed to prevent a student from enrolling for a school's summer Arabic immersion camp in Morocco, for instance. Furthermore, the acceptance of credit for such experiences (if any is offered by the home institution at all) can be a time-consuming process requiring patience and advocacy. As students are further connected through technology and globalization, it becomes increasingly imperative that schools and communities value the skills taught through cross-cultural education and strive to provide meaningful experiences that help shape open-minded and culturally aware citizens.

As the economy becomes more global in nature, schools and institutions of higher learning must also reflect that diversity and become communities of learners who recognize and appreciate the skills and perspectives gained from engaging in cross-cultural learning experiences. Evidence has suggested that cultural immersion programs, whether through long-term programs, such as a study abroad, or short-term programs, such as cultural exchange or service trips, provide students with a number of benefits, both academic and personal. With technology in distance learning improving, cross-cultural learning is no longer an adjunct to formal schooling. For example, schools have begun utilizing videoconferencing technology to connect students from around the world to help teach and learn alongside other. Formal schools are establishing formal links or on occasion formal campuses in other countries, drawing upon a network of schools and teachers to provide cross-cultural learning experiences to an increasing number of students. One program in particular, International Baccalaureate (IB), an international education foundation known for its rigorous, inquiry-based curricula, has over 900,000 students in 140 countries enrolled, and as the number of IB programs and students grow, it is expected that formal, cross-cultural learning experiences will become more common.

4.3. Global Projects and Partnerships

Some of the main actions being performed by these organizations and governments are working on equal rights and opportunities for gender and ethnic minorities, contributing to the estimation and collection of more reliable and accurate data, and working with governments to implement effective policies and provide accessible and equitable education for all. In 2018, the World Bank Group announced a new Human Capital Index—a tool for measuring and assessing the future potential of countries' population. Countries with higher human capital scores are expected to have higher long-term per capita GDP growth, considering that they will generate a population able to achieve and maintain competitive status within the global economy. Aiming for higher scores in the Human Capital Index and addressing the importance of investing in human capital, the Sub-Saharan Africa region was encouraged to enroll every child to develop seamless access to education and improve learning conditions, among other strategic investments. The challenge of achieving the education SDG therefore cuts across many global concerns.

There are many funds, initiatives, and partnerships involved in helping to solve global education and SDG 4 challenges. Achieving the education goal of the SDG is a big challenge that requires the participation of all stakeholders. Several philanthropic organizations are also involved in contributing to the realization of the education goals. Some of the main philanthropic organizations participating in providing better educational opportunities all around the globe are the Bill & Melinda Gates Foundation, the Wellcome Trust, the Omidyar Network, the Lemann Foundation, Dubai Cares, Google.org (among others), and many private ones. The United Nations Educational, Scientific and Cultural Organization (UNESCO), in collaboration with many other organizations, is also involved in this noble mission.

5

Project-Based Learning

Originally, project-based learning was thought of as another class activity that could be used by a teacher to help students practice the cognitive skills presented in a lecture (also known as the direct instruction model or the sage-on-the-stage approach). An enthusiastic teacher can guide students through inquiry or discussion and then assign a project. However, students are usually not exposed to the ultimate goal for their learning as a result of the project until the beginning of the learning unit. Therefore, the project is a low-level application of information that does not allow students to contextualize their learning (skills) in a different context or transfer it to a new situation.

Project-based learning is an approach to learning that focuses on engaging students in an authentic, real-world context. It can take a few days or, in some cases, weeks. Participants are required to make small tangible deliverables, usually in the form of artifacts such as portfolios, that demonstrate their understanding of the concept being taught. Project-based learning is not for the SATs or AP exams. It is frequently confused with hands-on, experiential, or extended learning. However, project-based learning is not only about engaging students or even active learning. The real focus of project-based learning is to design units of study in such a way that students are not only practicing the cognitive skills that will be assessed.

5.1. Real-World Problem Solving

A final way educators can prepare students is to incorporate problem-based learning, which is generally found at the other end of the continuum from direct instruction. Its origins stretch back to the Middle Ages when medical students learned by solving a clinical problem. In 1969, Myron F. Steinman, a physician and professor, developed the problem-based learning model that is now implemented in medical schools throughout the world. With this method, school desks and textbooks are replaced with real-life problems that need solving. The theory behind the system is that students, when working scientifically, acquire better information comprehension and recall skills compared to students who learn more traditionally. With all that is currently happening in schools—namely the incorporation of technology, personalized learning, and active learning with a host of other innovations—only one thing is for certain: school as we remember it will not be the same. As such, readers are once again reminded to keep their minds open as they read through the title's individual chapters.

Not every student benefits from traditional, one-size-fits-all educational methods in which everyone learns the same way and at the same rate. One alternative solution rests in the hands of teachers. Given numerous instructional demands, educators are sometimes left without time to adjust their methods to suit each student's needs. In response to this issue, computer-based adaptive learning systems provide each student with an individualized learning path that allows them to be challenged when they are ready, make mistakes, and ultimately learn from them. Likewise, with so much data available through everything from demographics to biometrics, schools can create customized lessons and programs for each student.

5.2. Collaborative Projects

Some recent school or classroom designs recognize the importance of collaboration for critical thinking and group problem solving. For example, one middle school general education classroom in rural North Carolina has transformed any "wall" that exists in the classroom into "smart walls." When needed, the teacher can lower the wall to create learning areas in which small groups of children can collaborate using technology like smart boards. Emphasizing the importance of collaborative project work in mathematics class, an associate professor of mathematics at Anderson University argues that "the skill sets that support each other when solving authentic, complex problems can then be transferred to other settings, including mathematical theorizing and problem-solving."

There is a growing body of empirical evidence demonstrating the potential of educational technology to foster collaboration, including numerous case studies and surveys of existing practices. Increased educational possibilities that support increased levels of collaboration, whether they arise from educational technologies, new classroom designs or new pedagogical approaches, are mostly positive. New possibilities for collaboration within the class or school are especially promising if we hope for all children to have ready access to learning opportunities that develop their higher-order thinking abilities. Since most relevant outcomes of education like problem solving, critical thinking, metacognition, creativity, emotional intelligence, and cognitive complexity are difficult and expensive to measure and thus probably hard to incentivize effectively in markets, it is important that educational policies be designed to alleviate, rather than exacerbate, potential inequalities in students' access to educational opportunities that support the attainment of these outcomes.

5.3. Exhibition and Presentation of Learning

These emerging trends and the factors driving those trends provide a promising picture for the future of education. If Lasallian educators are prepared and able to lead, we can reshape the future in this unique and still-in-formation landscape of personal, digital, flattened, decoupled, and recombined educational opportunity. The Lasallian voice will be heard and play an important role.

- Provide experiences that put students first. - Expand real-world interdisciplinary programs, like Project Based Learning and Challenge Based Learning. - Embrace experiential teaching processes like Result-Based Schooling and help all students develop the capacity to be lifelong learners. - Treat all students as unique individuals with unique gifts and challenges. - Ensure that every action of the school shows respect for every student and every aspect of the school, be they academic or non-academic. - Reduce emphasis on standardization and displays of traditional academic prowess and replace it with a focus on market-relevant learning. - Use consulting and advisement systems and counselor internships to help students identify potential applications for their unique gifts.

Trends shaping tomorrow's schools, such as deeper learning, personalized learning, and digital and blended learning, are redefining how we think of educational delivery. A new environment of education is needed, one that is characterized by what I refer to as student-centered, experiential, interdisciplinary, respectful, and market-relevant models. To implement this new model, Lasallians must:

6

Social and Emotional Learning

Research has shown that children who grow up in adverse conditions – due to poverty, environmental challenges, abuse, or a number of other factors – face outcomes in terms of mental and physical well-being that are significantly worse than those who grow up in more stable environments. In these conditions, a whole child approach is even more essential. Children who are either already traumatized or who are living in environments that are rife with risk need education environments that don't simply focus on drill and skill growth. They need support, skill building, empathetic mentorship, and in some cases more robust medical, nutritional, and mental health interventions to have a fighting chance at becoming successful adults. Even as this need exists, significant threats are converging to undermine educators' ability to construct the types of learning environments that provide essential social and emotional growth opportunities.

The development of the whole child – intellectually, socially, emotionally, and ethically – has always been a priority of education; indeed, it's been the primary focus for much of its history. Educators today need to pay more than mere lip service to teaching the whole child and to crafting learning environments that are responsive to the particular developmental needs of young people. Providing powerful, personally meaningful learning experiences, as well as an array of forms of support and social and emotional skill building that young people need to respond to the anxiety that arises from the growing uncertainty, inequality, and divisiveness in the United States and the world, must be seen as essential to the mission of every school teacher and administrator.

6.1. Emotional Intelligence Development

The Collaborative for Academic, Social, and Emotional Learning (CASEL), as cited in the George Lucas Education Foundation (GLEF) article "What is Social Emotional Learning?" suggests that programs that nurture "social and emotional learning (SEL) help [students] improve motivation to learn, better focus on and pay attention to others, and relate with other people. These skills work together to lead to positive social interactions and relationships, cooperative problem-solving, a more compassionate communication style, and good decision making" (Reksten). Indeed, social and emotional learning produces numerous benefits for students, including, but not limited to: improved communication and relationships with others, not limited to peers; increased dedication to learning; lessened disciplinary problems and bullying tendencies; and a higher capacity for problem-solving, including an enhanced ability to think critically and creatively.

As articulated by the organization Six Seconds, emotional intelligence (called "EQ") refers to the capacity for recognizing our own feelings and those of others, for motivating ourselves, and for managing emotions well in ourselves and in our relationships. Employers increasingly prioritize soft skills when hiring and promoting staff, identifying emotional intelligence as essential for career advancement. Fortunately, social-emotional learning (SEL) in schools can help students to develop emotional intelligence as well as social competence. Cary Cherniss and Daniel Goleman, two experts in EI, each espouse the importance of schools in nurturing emotional intelligence in learners who may otherwise struggle to understand the complexities of personal relationships. In an article titled "Emotional Intelligence: What It Is and Why It Matters," Goleman writes, "Children in school need support in gaining the social skills of cooperating, helping, sharing, and being aware of others' feelings…what we are talking about is emotional and social intelligence, the capacity to effectively manage ourselves and our relationships."

6.2. Mindfulness and Well-being

The rise of mindfulness and well-being in schools is illustrative of the increasing importance parents and educators place on children's mental health, not just their cognitive development. With mental health problems growing at such a rapid pace, it is clear that current approaches to intervention, though well-intended, are not far-reaching enough. While school counseling programs, focused on an individual level, attempt to mitigate these effects, they cannot hope to reach the many young students already grappling with mental health corrosion—nor can these programs address the societal pressures that likely contribute to the increased occurrence of mental distress. These societal pressures, the unintended and troubling byproducts of the equal-success-for-all fiat, have taken a toll on students. For this reason, teachers need to be trained on how to address mental health in schools. Mindfulness and well-being programs will perhaps give them the best tools to engage in this area, aside from formal therapy.

Being a teacher has become a highly stressful job. Teachers, once revered for nurturing future generations, are now tasked with fostering test-takers. Students are not the only ones suffering the impacts of stress in education. In the US, one of the leading contributors to teacher attrition is the desire to leave the profession due to working conditions. To keep teaching professionals healthy—and in the classroom—administrators and boards should consider the well-being of teachers. One emerging solution in both educational and professional settings is the practice of mindfulness. Research has shown that even short-term interventions in classroom settings can decrease levels of stress and burnout and increase teaching efficacy. At the same time, mindfulness has been identified as a catalyst for exploration, critical thinking, and understanding, making teachers better at their job.

6.3. Building Positive Relationships

Personalization is not only a pedagogical concept but an entirely social phenomenon. Developing understanding and empathy are key limiting factors in establishing good relationships, but technologies will also help. Advances in emotion recognition, for example, can immediately convey voice tone, comment, and feeling to students who may be more anxious about the new school environment or from students who were less attentive in online learning but are now teachers in person. To help students learn more effectively and allow educators to support more students on an individual basis, adaptive learning is a necessity of our educational approach. In reaction to non-negotiable social and emotional components, we realize that the adaptive learning software needs to develop to recognize, acknowledge, and appropriately answer the mechanisms of social interaction among students and educators.

For many students, their teachers are some of their main sources of support, mentorship, and guidance. As educators, we understand the responsibility of supporting our students and the long-term gains that positive relationships bring. One of the biggest opportunities points to better ways for students and educators to connect, as well as advancements in data systems and the broader data landscape that increase opportunities for educationally significant interactions, news, and recommendations. The guiding principle behind these technological innovations is strengthening the role of objective data and personalized insights. Tech developers are building digital solutions that help students, educators, families, and schools collect meaningful data to support student success.

7

STEAM Education

If one of your goals of STEM education is to break the recent trends of inequity in gender, race, ethnicity, and socioeconomic status in the area of these disciplines, then it also includes the arts. In 2010, John Maeda, President of Rhode Island School of Design, came up with the concept of the essential relationship of art and design to science, technology, engineering, and math in a move to broaden public support for arts education. "Not only can the arts increase the quality of a STEM education, this way of thinking visits why creativity matters, and what can be done to maintain that spirit in the face of the systemized regimentation which tends to industrialize the arts," states Maeda. Since this time, it has gained traction partially because student experiences in public school are divided along strict subject lines, often illustrated through timelines that follow specific subject matter exposure over a child's life.

Steam is an acronym for science, technology, engineering, arts, and mathematics. This interdisciplinary approach connects each of these subjects, which are found through explicit instruction, inquiry, and cross-disciplinary projects. The focus on these areas is intended to prepare students for high-demand jobs that require computing science as well as the skills developed through collaborative, creative endeavors, and critical thinking. The goal of STEM education is to attract more students, including women and underrepresented minority groups, to these subjects. Through an increased focus on career connections, STEM educators focus on the application of learning, often through project-based methods. These foundational skills are a perfect match for the skills we know students will need in order to succeed in the future. To keep the curriculum focused on the future, STEAM education encourages dialogue around what the roles of science, technology, engineering, and mathematics look like when they come together to nurture the skills of the future.

7.1. Integration of Arts and Design

In response to better prepare students for the modern era, this practice will produce a resulting generation of modern artists and students primed with the technology required for the 21st century. Researchers and educators working on the incorporation of the arts and design into the core curriculum have found that teaching them only in school and college would not have a long-term effect. In order to be efficient, however, the schools would have to treat them as equivalent subjects to math and sciences and also commit equal resources to them: lesson hours, educator training, and checking the outcomes of the courses.

The notion of including art and design in education might seem unusual. In order to succeed in the modern era, the ability to be inquisitive, innovative, and imaginative is essential to building the range of skill sets required for the 21st century. Art and design exist to challenge our traditional notions, expectations, and perspectives, and therefore they need to become part of the K-12 curriculum. The demand for integration of subjects is inevitable. Educators must evolve by actively connecting core and integrated subjects to more poorly understood and less formal public skills such as creativity, design, and interest in the arts.

Successful Incorporation of Arts and Design

7.2. Focus on Science, Technology, Engineering, and Mathematics

Science should be contacted by an experienced person with scientific studies to appeal to young people. Educators will need to be a part of continuous science learning. Possessiveness is necessary with more frequent attention conducive to increased success. Moosgeeter advocated that 27 states offer only one-year service preparation to teach middle school science. Advancing in the pioneering scientific process will generate an approach to technology that: a) relates scientific concepts to technology; b) A School dialog acts as a catalyst for interest in technological concepts, as well as the need to know concepts and principles, within students who must invent. Digital integration allows the provision of resources, questions, and challenges that are vital. c) It allows interested student use of universal support materials in the technological field; d) empowers teachers and students to face technological challenges in real life situations, through the scientific method.

As with many of the proposals here, ADE must be involved in the implementation of the Mathematize It! Methodology. They should also design projects with access to magnifying glasses that can be used in any curricular area. The gift of Iridescent Science provides digital kits and lessons to guide students in engineering projects that address everything from human need to scientific principles. In general, today's methods for teaching the concept of design must be modified. The STEM experience must extend through high school; and to ensure this, college students should receive instruction from educators who have degrees in the traditional basic areas. Elementary educators graduate with multiple credits in science and countless professional secretions as science majors with no science experience.

Educators must determine what knowledge and skills all students need to possess. Consequently, an updated curriculum enabling students to exploit digital access will be created for the profession of the future. Just as there are global standards for basic education, young students must learn to become capable of global communication and problem solving through Project-Based Learning, and the use of the design or scientific methodology. This requires students to focus on integrating science, technology, engineering, and mathematics (STEM). It is important that the technological cross-disciplinary nature of the basic concepts in each area is not lost.

7.3. Creativity and Innovation

The words "newly recognized" point to a change in what we see as creativity. Parents and teachers regularly resonate that "this is not the way work" or "this is not how one would write an assignment" in a quest to stop their, from their perspective, non-creative and non-innovative children from being imaginative. One of the questions that continues to provoke discussion is whether Tim Berners-Lee could have invented the World Wide Web if he had been subjected to too much "education." That is, both parents and teachers strive to discipline children to become "educated" as they perceive it to be the way to success, and they frequently try to do this by curbing the resourceful activities that could enhance creativity and innovation in the future.

Are educators fostering the seeds of creativity or, as Ken Robinson represents it, "educated" in the opposite? How can we teach in a way that enhances creativity? What are the criteria for creative tasks? This section discusses creativity as it is one of the most commonly cited future skill demands in the fifty-two texts listed. Typical for educational research, creativity is defined and measured in a plethora of ways. talk about the rise of the creative class, as well as the divergence between the creative and the "non-recognized" jobs. He says that "creativity has been newly recognized by the economic development community as vital to enhancing the quality of our life, and a diverse range of city-based measures of creativity draw intense interest".

Creativity has its roots in childhood, but argues for a new era of creativity in education, where children are equipped to be creative, innovative, flexible mental scientists and engineers, and to understand the intersection of art and science as prime movers of the spirit of the time and as a result of human intelligence. Creativity and innovation are also one of last year's global trends in the 2015 NMC Horizon report, while creativity is listed as one of the top three important skills for future employees, a trend signaled as early as 2010 in reports such as The Future of Work.

8

Future Skills Development

To begin, companies need to have a clear understanding of the advanced technologies that are booming. In the end, however, it is humans who impart their intelligence (aptitudes, capabilities, and talents) to machines and systems based on advanced technologies to develop new features and find applications. With increasingly effective advanced technologies, an extended workforce (managers, professionals, and freelancers) will cultivate and apply their own unique skills, potentiating the use of rapidly evolving tools in new and more complex roles. This encourages us to renew the way we cultivate the capacity for learning and creativity in our extended workforce, which is crucial to humanize these technologies and channel them towards generating economic and scalable benefits. To carry out this initiative, the demand for essential technologies and capabilities will emerge at all levels of job competition, a process that will empower the extended workforce, encouraging companies to reposition their employees and redefine employee career phases. In the future, the triumphant companies of the Fourth Industrial Revolution will have to rely not only on advanced technologies but also on extended talent and an environment that promotes continuous growth, learning, and change.

In the 21st century, we see an increasing trend in changing the skills of the future workforce. While automation and artificial intelligence will displace jobs, many new roles will be created at the intersection between technology and people—roles that we can barely imagine today. Mobility will redefine the skills needed in certain types of work and promote entirely new business models. In a world in which automation systems and robotics, freelancers will also have to be more flexible and will have to anticipate changes, so companies will need skills to maneuver effectively in complex contexts and to become better at constant change and uncertainty. The technology, combined with demand, will allow the design of adaptable and individualized structures to the task of people, leading to constant professional growth of the workers. Companies, especially those in the US and Europe, should take advantage of this moment to improve the formation and productive potential of the workers. In Europe, the percentage of unemployed individuals or not integrated into the labor market, or people who are in extremely precarious conditions and who do not carry out a professional activity or who receive a pension, has reached 10%. These individuals should be invested in training for life or be in requalified programs to adapt their skills and gain access to the formation of Industry 4.0.

8.1. Critical Thinking and Problem Solving

The NEA report "Tomorrow's Schools" evaluated 20 top experts and concluded that the most necessary curricular emphasis across the nation is on critical and analytical thinking ability. Jean-François Rischard, Vice President for Europe at the World Bank and author of "High Noon: 20 Global Problems, 20 Years to Solve Them," amplifies the urgency in an interview, saying, "Over the longer term, the only way to go for education is to cultivate this very important trait of curiosity and hence critical thinking, problem-solving, and figuring things out for yourself. The world is changing so fundamentally that no one, I believe, can be optimistic about the prospects of economies that are not fostered on creating jobs that are about thinking, that are about imagination, where people are engaged in entrepreneurship." As workers, critical thinkers are a premium in any establishment.

The word "critical" comes from the Greek word meaning "to sift or separate." When we think critically, we are sifting and separating the bad from the good, the fact from the fiction, the plausible from the spurious. Critical thinking is not simply about thinking thoughts, but about thinking thoughts through, using intellectual criteria in the process. According to Richard Paul, a key figure in the critical thinking movement, critical thinking is an intellectual process that requires disciplined use of the mind because it comes from the Greek word meaning "to sift or separate." Critical thinkers don't merely say what they think or feel, but use criteria and standards to examine, test, categorize, prioritize, analyze, interpret, and contextualize observations and experiences in order to identify self-deception or "other-trickery." For this reason, among top-tier colleges and universities, the cultivation of critical thinking is emerging as a desired educational outcome.

8.2. Collaboration and Communication

As the push towards transparency and flattening organizations persists in industry, the question of what role educators play in this movement inevitably arises. Should the teacher be central, like the expert in an industry publication or as a presenter at a large conference? Should the classroom or lab be the primary work of the teacher, engaging a much larger audience online or in a distance education-like model? To move with industry or societal trends, what role is played by the educator? Many existing industrial models put the teacher at the center of the classroom. Are such structures the best mechanism to teach the habits and skills that will be greatly needed in the future? Or are existing structural models convenient and, therefore, should remain in spaces that are not always conducive to such changes?

There are two primary themes that emerge in terms of communication among and between learners and educators in a rapidly changing learning environment: personalization and collaboration. As anonymity becomes more difficult to achieve, greater communication becomes not only more likely but also, potentially, more meaningful. Personalization becomes a critical piece of new learning models. To many, this seems counterintuitive as, historically, the schoolhouse has been as much an assimilation as a differentiation mechanism. The need for personalization has, historically, been one of convenience. Now, the need for personalization is one borne out of necessity.

8.3. Adaptability and Resilience

The advent of the most recent digital era has forcefully brought forth the concept of online learning as a viable solution to providing open access to the highest levels of education. The most recent beta tests of educational technology showcase the potential benefits of more personalized, technology-driven, global educational experiences. Media coverage and marketing for such programs display features of 21st-century learning, including authentic tasks and collaboration, with the goal of preparing students for further technological advancements that directly shape the future. This thesis suggests bridging our current divide by increasing hybrid learning technologies in traditional educational programs. Modern definitions of hybrid learning suggest that these programs should be centered on the unique needs of a modern student body, allowing adaptation based on the evolution of knowledge. Proposals to universally modernize educational models are tested and found to offer substantial potential for increasing student learning outcomes and increasing widespread access to the transference of 21st-century skills.

Adolescent growth and development are indicating a developing need for new approaches to learning. In youth and young adults, a growing recognition of the importance of skills like adaptability and resilience marks an increase in awareness of the changing nature of work. Common learning environments today are formal, non-flexible programs that emphasize academic content and achievement for a future they often inadequately prepare students for, consistently failing to ensure that they are ready to enter the workforce. A potential solution to better prepare students for genuine future success lies in expanded learning that emphasizes modern soft skills as students learn new content and skills. By emphasizing these characteristics, learners would develop competence in life and career readiness skills through crowd-sourced learning experiences. As a result of practicing such skills through real-life challenges, learners should be better equipped to apply themselves in their future personal and professional endeavors, making the benefits of state schooling available throughout a lifetime and the workforce.

9

Inclusive Education

The advantages of inclusive education are numerous. It makes possible the education of students in the normal school environment, which eventually develops the capacity to understand and respect individual differences, and helps in the identification of special needs, employing the necessary support to develop adequate solutions. An inclusive approach can thus raise standards in schools and improve the attainment of students. It can prepare students for successful transition from school to further study, employment, and independent living. Inclusive education is important for promoting the education of students with disabilities and establishing egalitarian education. Students go to school not just to learn the "three Rs," that is, "Reading, Writing, Arithmetic"; they will go as well to develop cultural values, to interact socially, to build interests, and to foster personal development and independent lives. This is what is meant by the United Nations Educational, Scientific, and Cultural Organization (UNESCO) when proposing, in its 2008 "Policy Guidelines on Inclusion in Education," that an inclusive approach stimulates respect and recognition of diversity and "fosters social cohesion and democratic values."

Inclusive education is generally seen as sending a positive message and having the advantage of leading all educational staff, policy developers, parents, and the general public to believe that all students belong in school and have a right to an appropriate education. A simple definition of inclusive education is that it is an educational approach that aims to embrace all students. Schools employing such an approach welcome all students regardless of disability, race, gender, sexual orientation, religion, or nationality and organize the education of students in ways that respond to the students' abilities. An inclusive education policy is a means to facilitate the realization of the right to education for all learners. It is a matter that should be considered in the development of international agendas and policies. Inclusive education is a right and should be available and accessible to all students.

9.1. Special Needs Support

Finally, amid all these new directions shaping the future, it is essential to understand that years ago, many elderly people (educators and non-educators alike) insisted that no "real" change had occurred in the system that punched out teachers just like they themselves had been punched. One morning, though, addressing a class of practicing teachers at the midpoint of a week-long workshop, I shared a student's mother's observation. She had been a little girl in the Ocala National Forest when Marjorie Kinnan Rawlings had just bought her house in Cross Creek, and every so often this writer would walk neighbors' children to catch the school bus. One day, little Ruth held her book to her chest, as if holding Marjorie Kinnan Rawlings' thoughts and dreams close to her heart, and asked if meeting anyone of fame just took having a dream as extra special as Mrs. Rawlings'. Eyeing the little girl with her eyes wide open, the author said, "Go to school. Just make sure it's not far from your childhood dreams."

Not so very long ago, infusing special needs students into the general education classroom was, in itself, a hot trend in certain schools. However, these same students invariably suffered from the "vodka principle," as I used to call it, seeing as how putting them in the same classes as the general education students didn't automatically lead to "shaken, not stirred" friendships. But with the newest special needs trend, those students are the ones de rigueur, and only by becoming part of the general education scene can educators help students who might otherwise be marginalized in separate programs that aren't as easily monitored. In fact, recognizing the need for designated support but with the ultimate goal of infusing special needs students into the general education classroom, many innovative models have appeared, among them co-teaching teams (a general education teacher and special education teacher sharing a general education classroom) or special education teachers serving as consultant or resource in a general education classroom while tending at the same time to their own special needs students. Another model is the concept of the full-time special education teacher acting as a case manager as well as support team for special needs students being "pushed in" to a general education classroom, and while created for students with only mild disabilities, this model has recently been implemented with those having moderate to severe ones.

9.2. Diversity and Equity

Requiring expensive laptops and digital resources, remote learning has already increased the social gap among students. Lower-income families tend to share one device among family members and were less likely to have home internet access or reliable broadband network. Data from UNICEF showed that 463 million students around the world had no access to remote learning during last year, while 258 million were affected by network rigidities and lack of infrastructure. The results indicated that girls were more affected than boys, including at the governmental policy level. For girls living in extremely poor countries, the pandemic responses were 23% less generous than for boys as well. In most countries, girls are at higher risk of domestic abuse, child marriage, unplanned pregnancies, sexual violence, and early school abandonment.

As schools across the world move to remote learning, many questions remain about how education may change as a result of the coronavirus pandemic. For now, however, we are seeing a sector in crisis, with many children from disadvantaged backgrounds underserved. In the long run, government intervention may increase funding for digital education, as well as home internet access. Also, irrespective of the type of school, adequate teacher training, funding for digital resources, and personal support for students and their families may be essential in the medium-to-long term. Under these circumstances, the various innovative teaching and learning models that have emerged are revealing essential strengths and weaknesses, as well as good practices that can be celebrated, supported, and scaled. To minimize the impact inflicted by the pandemic on the teaching/learning process, educational publishers are coming up with various alternatives to traditional education, while also proposing specific solutions.

9.3. Universal Design for Learning

The UDL model has three main tools. The first tool states that information should be presented in a variety of ways to enhance its effectiveness. This text can also provide multiple representations of the same concepts to support learning. The second tool is that the learning environment should offer a variety of activities that can help students increase their engagement level and keep them motivated. In order to eliminate the need for on-the-spot decisions that can lead to bias and restricting students' access, algorithms learned from trace data of how students learn can help instructors determine whether or not the student has put in a sufficient amount of effort and motivation. The third tool highlights that instructors should allow a variety of methods for students to express what they know. In order to help students evaluate their work and to sharpen skills needed for them to provide useful feedback, algorithms providing trace data analysis can allow instructors to provide constructive criticism in a timely manner and provide a framework for improvement.

One way to foster equity and remove barriers to learning is to create educational experiences that are accessible and beneficial for everyone. Universal Design for Learning (UDL) is an educational framework that encourages designing educational experiences that can accommodate a diverse group of students by including options and flexibility within the curriculum, in order to effectively remove barriers in the environment, in the task, and in how students are motivated and engaged. This type of learning could remove the need for the traditional model that separates out students for instruction and instead promote a "one-size-fits-one" learning opportunity. An alternative model for UDL in the classroom is a personalized learning experience with holistic support offering the services of individualized education programs (IEPs), computer-based education, and flexible, competency-based systems to meet the needs of all students, including those with learning disabilities. Nevertheless, in a survey of more than 800 teachers, 61% reported that they had not integrated any form of the framework into their teaching practices. Educators argue that the UDL model can only work for motivated and skilled students. To some extent, UDL's guidelines can increase the complexity of instruction and its use in practical settings.

10

Teacher Professional Development

Professional development effect size of 0.50 indicates a substantial impact for changes in digital-era skill development. Professional development in this area, tailored to account for different target student populations and delivered in ways to maximize cost-efficiency, could be the most impactful way to use the billions of hours available in teachers' potential cloud use. The most effective professional development to improve teaching and learning is likely to be consistent with the individual teacher's needs and the teacher's own interest in personalized digital learning platforms for teaching, teacher network project collaboration outside the traditional school day, digital learning communities, collaborations with visiting scholars who interact with teachers and their students, industry pro bono participation in the local educational environment, and other strategies that tap smart taxes of 1% on teachers' time and work week and existing philanthropic investments. Benefit-to-cost ratios for the investments in this area are likely to be very favorable, take little additional funding, and should be carefully scrutinized by both nonprofit educators and public policymakers.

There is little chance to achieve the potential of educational clouds without nurturing not only the success of students but also the adaptability of the schools and their staffs. Opportunities for professional development are evolving to increase teacher adaptability. Participating in pro bono work in areas relevant to teaching and learning can hone teacher skills and help teachers expand networks outside schools to learn and share useful ideas digitally and face-to-face. In addition, professional development is expected to shift from in-service workshops to various forms of online learning. Despite current limitations and slow uptake of policies and programs, over the next years, teachers are expected to regularly engage in at least some ongoing digital learning that earns them digital badges and micro-credentials for new competencies. Unbundled, stackable forms of micro-credential training will confer the most benefit when they can eventually be applied to earning more formal, traditionally career-advancing units, such as masters' and doctoral degrees, and such transitions will need increasingly digital licensing, satisfaction of the requirements via digital learning, e-portfolios of relevant work, and other digital processes that document skills and competencies. Policymakers will increasingly recognize that current misaligned incentives, standards, and management systems greatly inhibit educational cloud developments and actively address them.

10.1. Continuous Learning Opportunities

Nine states so far have created modern "funding entitlements": portable accounts, regularly adjusted for inflation, that empower all students with choices that reflect individual needs, aptitudes, and aspirations. States award entitlements to someone's Ascent Education Investment Foundation account. An Ascent scholarship is awarded to supply what isn't in the account. Theportal.school becomes the biggest school because its average scholarship award buys all of a student's needed services. Dr. Piechowski and Dr. Nowicki in Poland - comparing standardized VTS 3 (Mastery of Progressive Academic Standards) tests against the standardized Proglo (Proficiency, Growth, Learning-Oriented) tests - found the DREs increased the learning of non-standard kids by six years in four years. Since we only counted kids in testing windows, the net improvement may be bigger still.

Rapid technological changes demand ever-new skills. Given this reality, states need to provide continuous learning opportunities. This is even tougher than it sounds because too many states use funding models designed for "in-seat" students: those that show up in a certain place for a certain time. Here's what happens: Suppose you have a non-working fifty-year-old needing new welding skills and a sixteen-year-old that needs teaching in tenth grade algebra. Today, a "school" gets state money for the sixteen-year-old, but none for the "non-standard" fifty-year-old. But this "non-standard" scenario increasingly defines everyone.

10.2. Technology Integration Training

In general, effective professional development supports teachers in their work with students by others and engagement of educators in curriculum development, the writing of performance goals, and the evaluation of student projects. It is critical for professional development to support the instantiation of technology-rich learning environments in education. Professional development should be ongoing, be delivered by mentors who are also educators, and provide support resources for educators as they integrate technology in their lessons. Professional development must not only be modeled by educators who are integrating technology in their teaching, but also by administrators and other professionals who will mentor emerging teachers and evaluators.

In most school settings, formal training for teachers on successful technology integration has, at best, been occasional, if it has existed at all. While "traditional" technology instruction often focused on teaching educators how to use specific technologies, effective integration in education has always been driven by curriculum and by a focus on students and learning. The most successful technology-using teachers have adopted teachers' technology practices and have implemented effective technology integration in the face of financial and technical constraints, while failing to implementies play a parallel role in their learning spaces, allowing them the same agency that students are expected to exert over their learning. A variety of strategies for fostering teachers' technology integration have been used in specific areas of instruction and have demonstrated great promise. Professional development experience, especially those involving the study of exemplars that demonstrate effective technology use, have also been found to be effective.

10.3. Pedagogical Innovations

Digital technologies can help teachers find the best artistic resources, connect with museum personnel, and create interpretative museum exhibitions demonstrating understanding linked to curricular goals like storytelling, time and place simulations, and interactive activities. By facilitating virtual field trips (VFTs), professional learning for teachers, and specific curricular resources through a number of teacher-based inquiries, they have been able to support the adoption of humanized and meaningful learning practices.

Museums and galleries can provide valuable resources to support interdisciplinary and project-based learning. Museums are rich with primary source artifacts, and galleries excite through direct encounters with original art objects. Institutions often use key questions to define the parameters of a unit, and then use related and supporting inquiries to scaffold new learning opportunities.

At the middle and high school levels, problem-based and project-based learning allows students to grapple with important, relevant issues. Sometimes guided by digital technologies, but often through the real-world application of more traditional skills. The development and evaluation of evaluative rubrics is an essential skill both in museums and galleries (especially in the visual arts) and for digital citizens.

A vast majority of interesting and independent work not only provides students with opportunities for customization and creative choice, but takes advantage of the affordances of digital tools to expand learning opportunities. Importantly, these types of projects tend to promote deeper learning (learning that involves going beyond simple recall of information and that is related to meaningful assessment). Projects that allow for the most open creative processes and offer students more choices seem to correlate with more learning.

Milton Keynes UK
Ingram Content Group UK Ltd.
UKHW031352011224
451755UK00004B/364